Field Trips

At the Nature Center

By Sophie Geister-Jones

www.littlebluehousebooks.com

Little Blue House is distributed by North Star Editions:
sales@northstareditions.com | 888-417-0195

Produced for Little Blue House by Red Line Editorial.

Photographs ©: IPGGutenbergUKLtd/iStockphoto, cover; Rawpixel/iStockphoto, 4; dtokar/iStockphoto, 6–7; yorkfoto/iStockphoto, 9 (top); Marc Belair/iStockphoto, 9 (bottom); kali9/iStockphoto, 10 (top); Sean Xu/Shutterstock Images, 10 (bottom); Lighthouse Photography/iStockphoto, 13, 24 (bottom right); john shepherd/iStockphoto, 14–15; Eileen Kumpf/iStockphoto, 17; KenCanning/iStockphoto, 18, 20–21, 23, 24 (top left), 24 (top right), 24 (bottom left)

Library of Congress Control Number: 2019908622

ISBN
978-1-64619-032-4 (hardcover)
978-1-64619-071-3 (paperback)
978-1-64619-110-9 (ebook pdf)
978-1-64619-149-9 (hosted ebook)

Printed in the United States of America
Mankato, MN
012020

About the Author

Sophie Geister-Jones likes reading, spending time with her family, and eating cheese. She lives in Minnesota.

Table of Contents

At the Nature Center

We take a field trip to the nature center.

We want to see plants and animals.

The nature center has large fields and many trees.

We see a pond at the nature center.
A green frog jumps into the pond.

We See Bugs

We look for different kinds of bugs.

We try to catch butterflies in our nets.

We see a spider with eight legs.
The spider crawls in its sticky web.

A worm wiggles in the dirt. The worm will spend most of its time underground.

We see a
green grasshopper.
The grasshopper has
long legs that help it
jump high.

grasshopper

We See Animals

A skunk walks in

the grass.

It has a bushy tail.

A fawn is a baby deer.
The fawn runs through a
field of flowers.

An eagle flies high in the sky.
It is looking for small animals to eat.

Glossary

eagle

skunk

fawn

spider

Index